Toward A World Christian Fellowship

KENNETH SCOTT LATOURETTE
D. WILLIS JAMES PROFESSOR OF MISSIONS AND
ORIENTAL HISTORY IN YALE UNIVERSITY

Author of
A History of the Expansion of Christianity
A History of Christian Missions in China
The Chinese, Their History and Culture
Missions Tomorrow

Sixth Printing

Price 50 cents

HAZEN BOOKS ON RELIGION
The Edward W. Hazen Foundation, Inc.

Distributed by
ASSOCIATION PRESS
347 Madison Avenue
NEW YORK

A Note about
The Hazen Books on Religion

THE purpose of this series is to present simply, compactly, and inexpensively a number of the best available interpretations of the Christian philosophy as a guide to Christian living today.

The series is sponsored by the Edward W. Hazen Foundation. The responsibility for selecting the titles and authors and for planning the manufacture and distribution of the volumes rests with the following committee: John C. Bennett (chairman), Wilbur Davies, Georgia Harkness, S. M. Keeny, Benson Y. Landis, Mrs. W. W. Rockwell, William L. Savage, George Stewart, Henry P. Van Dusen, and a representative of the Edward W. Hazen Foundation. The responsibility for the subject matter of the volumes rests with the authors alone.

The following twelve volumes comprise the series:

Christianity—and Our World. By John C. Bennett. (Ten printings)

Jesus. By Mary Ely Lyman. (Eight printings)

God. By Walter Horton. (Five printings)

Religious Living. By Georgia Harkness. (Eight printings)

Toward a World Christian Fellowship. By Kenneth Scott Latourette. (Five printings)

Prayer and Workship. By Douglas Steere. (Six printings)

The Church. By George Stewart. (Three printings)

Christians in an Unchristian Society. By Ernest Fremont Tittle. (Three printings)

What Is Man? By Robert L. Calhoun. (Three printings)

Christian Faith and Democracy. By Gregory Vlastos. (Five printings)

The Bible. By Walter Russell Bowie. (Three printings)

Reality and Religion. By Henry P. Van Dusen. (Three printings)

The publication of these books is a co-operative, non-profit enterprise for everybody concerned.

CONTENTS

BY WAY OF INTRODUCTION

Is there any justification for attempting to make Christianity world wide? Is not one religion about as good as another? Does not each people in the course of time build up a religion adapted to its culture? Do not serious and unhappy dislocations follow when a folk of one cultural heritage abandons its inherited faith for another that has developed under a different set of circumstances? Have Christians any right to make "proselytes" from adherents of other religions? Is it not narrow-minded, provincial, arrogant, and impertinent to strive for a world-wide Christian fellowship? If we are to have a universal religion at all, should it not come out of a common search for truth? Ought not those of various religious traditions to pool what they think they have learned of ultimate reality, and without any assumption of superior insight embark, in a spirit of humility and of reciprocal sharing, upon a joint exploration of whatever may lie back of the religions of mankind?

Is not the dream of a world-wide Christian fellowship fantastic? From practically the beginning, the followers of Jesus have been divided. Though professing a religion whose primary precept for conduct is love, Christians have bitterly denounced and persecuted one another. They have been divided into many churches and denominations. To-day these divisions are more numerous than ever before. Within denominations and local congregations, outwardly united, dissensions are frequent. In light of these hard facts, is not any effort to create a world-wide fellowship that will include all Christians foredoomed to failure?

These are honest questions. They are asked by many intelligent people, including numbers of those who call themselves Christians.

It is partly to answers to these questions that the following pages are devoted.

The answers, like the questions, are honest. They are not meant to be argumentative. The issues are too basic and too important to be handled as an intellectual exercise or for the pleasure of debate. The welfare of hundreds of millions of individuals and the future of civilization and of the entire human race are involved. Anyone who attempts to deal with them seriously owes it to his fellows to face them with candor and with as much rigor and integrity of thought as he can command.

Yet answers, if they are to be frank and something more than superficial, must embody convictions. Even tentative replies and expressions of ignorance must be not careless, but positive, based upon an unhurried examination of the facts. No one can meditate long on any body of data without reaching certain conclusions. These may be tentative. They may be clear-cut affirmations. Common honesty, of course, demands that they be not blindly or stubbornly adhered to just because they have once been reached. One should always be ready to revise or even to discard his most cherished and basic beliefs if these be disproved by new facts or by fresh light on old facts. It is a false pride or a mistaken loyalty that seeks to maintain obstinately a position to which one has been publicly committed and which declines to look at it again open-mindedly from time to time, particularly if it be challenged by thoughtful people. However, a readiness to re-examine the principles on which one may have based his life does not preclude a quiet inward assurance of the validity of these principles or an unreserved dedication of all that one has to some cause. Indeed, an unwillingness to reopen a question may arise from a lurking fear that the foundations of one's faith will not bear scrutiny.

The following pages, then, are not a series of questions. They are made up chiefly of affirmations. They are an attempt at a forthright expression of convictions and hopes to which many are gladly devoting all that they have—of time, of ability, of reputation. Necessarily they are stated in summary fashion. The announced purpose of this series of little books excludes an elaborate treatise. To meet the purpose of the series, technical terminology has been shunned. What is said is being expressed in as clear and as simple language as possible. It is as though one were attempting, in a circle of friends in a long evening by the fire, to state unreservedly some of his most cherished dreams and at least some of the reasons for the faith that is in him.

A logical order in which to treat our topic seems to arrange itself as follows. (1) First we shall attempt to set forth the reasons for striving to develop a world-wide Christian fellowship. (2) Then we shall seek to discover the characteristics essential to such a fellowship. (3) We shall follow this with a description of the progress that is being made toward bringing into being a world-wide Christian fellowship. (4) That will be succeeded by an enumeration of the problems that must be solved if the dream of this fellowship is to come to full fruition. (5) Finally we shall seek to discover the next steps that are at once feasible and necessary if our generation is to make the progress toward this goal which can reasonably be expected.

CHAPTER I

A WORLD-WIDE CHRISTIAN FELLOWSHIP
IS IMPERATIVE

I

The basic conviction underlying these pages is that *we are living in an age that needs, and needs desperately, a growing world-wide Christian fellowship.* For this need there are two closely related reasons.

1. *A growing world-wide Christian fellowship is required for the spiritual and moral undergirding of the emerging world society.*

Ours is a day when recently invented mechanical appliances are rapidly drawing the human race physically together. The world is shrinking. Eighty years ago a hundred days by clipper ship was considered excellent time from New York to Canton, and for quick communication neither telephone nor telegraph was available. Now the distance is covered by air in almost as many hours, and telephonic and telegraphic communication between New York and China is practically instantaneous. Those of us still in middle life can recall the time when the dream of a Cape-to-Cairo railway was considered the last word for rapidity of transportation from the south to the north of Africa. Today regular air service brings the two extremes of the "Dark Continent" more closely together than would be possible by rail.

Not only is the size of the globe dwindling rapidly for communication and travel, but the earth is also being bound more closely together by the network of commerce. A simple breakfast table in New England may be supplied by bananas

1

from Central America, coffee from Brazil, sugar from Cuba, Hawaii, or the Philippines, and wheat or corn from the Middle West. After eating it, the business man may drive to his office in an automobile the rubber for whose tires came from the Malay Peninsula.

Rapid transportation and communication mean interdependence. The United States government, to placate a few western senators and an "inflationist bloc," embarks on a policy of purchasing silver at an enhanced price. One result is a financial crisis in silver-using China. Again, the depression reduces the price of silk in the American market. In consequence, Japanese farmers suffer, and their kindred in the army, seeking to relieve their plight, contribute to the elimination of Chinese rule in Manchuria and so help to precipitate a major international incident. Or, Gandhi starts a non-co-operative movement in India and thousands of workers are thrown out of employment in the cotton mills of Lancashire.

All this intercommunication and interdependence mean the emergence of the externals of a world culture. The mechanical appliances by which man has mastered his physical environment and increased his physical comfort are in use the world around. Practically every land and peoples of almost every culture use the telegraph, the telephone, and the automobile, and go to the cinema. The scientific processes that have made the machine possible are common property. In the great majority of countries, regardless of race, schools are teaching physics, chemistry, biology, engineering, medicine, and principles of agriculture. These techniques and branches of knowledge know no national boundaries, and they are essentially the same regardless of the background of the student's parents and grandparents. Historic cultures have not ceased to exist, but they are being profoundly altered by this common body of knowledge and these universally used appliances. In its physical tools and in the science that gives rise to them, mankind is increasingly one.

Yet, although in point of time-distance and of its basic appliances the planet is becoming a neighborhood, it is more and more a quarrelsome neighborhood. The very existence of civilization is threatened by international conflicts on a gigantic scale. The emerging world culture may be destroyed before it passes its infancy. This is in part because proximity, unless offset by some counter force, promotes friction. Peoples who, when they were too remote from one another for close intercourse, could live at peace, now that they are thrown closely together in a shrinking world are chronically at swords' points.

The difficulty is chiefly in the area of the spirit and of the mind. It is mainly in the realm of ideas that conflict arises. Dissension is bred by rival nationalisms based upon the now hazardous concept of national sovereignty, and by theories of the state and of economic organization that have become identified with particular nationalisms. We are told that the "democratic" nations must be prepared to stand against "totalitarian" nations, that between national socialism as embodied in Germany and communism as exemplified in Russia an irreconcilable conflict exists, and that Japan, rallying loyally around her Emperor and the imperial idea as represented by the ruling house, is threatened by communism in Russia and in Nationalist China. The peace movement, so strong in Anglo-Saxon lands, is largely impotent because it is not paralleled by peace movements in other lands. Tension is not primarily the outcome of economic competition—between "satisfied" and "unsatisfied" nations. Otherwise, Switzerland, Denmark, Norway, or Sweden would be loudly demanding colonies and access to raw materials and markets. It is primarily because of differing theories of the manner in which economic problems are to be solved. It also partly arises out of "power politics," the struggle of rival states, re-enforced by Nationalism, for prestige and might.

What is needed is the acceptance the world around of a common body of ideas that will make of the planet a friendly and not an unfriendly neighborhood, and that will give a sufficient spiritual and moral foundation for the emerging world culture. A basic difficulty in the development of international law is the lack of general acceptance by all peoples of common ethical principles on which that law can be built. If mankind is to work together in friendly co-operation, the large majority of the human race must yield allegiance to ideals that make for that co-operation. Moreover, these ideals must be of such a character that the world culture incorporating them will enable men and women and society as a whole to rise fully to their inherent possibilities. They must be of a kind that will stimulate to continued wholesome growth and not end in arrested development and sterility.

It is the conviction of many that this common body of ideas and ideals, together with the dynamic for their realization, is to be found nowhere else so fully as in the Christian faith. To the reasons for this conviction we shall come in a moment. Many believe, too, that this faith can be best imparted through a world-wide fellowship, with strong units in every land and among every people, and with its individual members conscious of its world-embracing character.

2. *A world-wide Christian fellowship is demanded to meet the persistent needs of men.*

It is not only to this age of an emerging world-culture that Christianity has a message. It also has the most satisfying answers to questions that man, because of his very nature and because of the nature of the universe in which he finds himself, has been raising for centuries. Moreover, as far as we can now see, he will continue to raise them so long as he remains man and continues to live on this planet.

Is man an orphan in a universe of blind and purposeless matter and unintelligent, automatic force? Or is the universe malevolent? Or is it an illusion from which man must seek to free himself? Or is whatever lies back of or within the universe entirely beyond man's comprehension? Or is the universe, including man, the work of One who desires the highest welfare of men, with whom men may have fellowship, and in companionship with whom men attain their fullest stature and their true destiny? Does the grave end all? Do men and women, after physical death, live on only in the memory of their fellows and in the influences for good or for ill that they have set in motion while in the flesh? Or does personality continue to exist after the dissolution of the body with which it has here been so closely associated? If so, what is the nature of that continued existence? Is it to be dreaded and, if possible, avoided; or has it the possibility of enduring and growing richness? Why does suffering exist? Some of it obviously is here through no fault of men. Some of it, just as obviously, is here through men's acts. Why are men of such a nature that they can bring misery to themselves and to their fellows? Is there any way by which men can be freed from the evil thoughts and deeds that end in unhappiness and disaster? These and many other questions have been with men for thousands of years. As far back as our records enable us to go, we find at least some of them being asked by some men. They haunt men and women of every race and of every culture.

If, as the evidence goes to show, the universe is real and orderly, and not an illusion or a chaos, it must be possible to discern light on these questions, and to approach satisfactory replies. To be valid, the answers must hold good for all men. Its expression may change, but in its essence the truth will not alter radically with the age, or with the climate of opinion, or with the culture. It is the conviction of many that Christianity has the most nearly satisfactory answers, and that these answers are best transmitted and, indeed, can be transmitted only through some kind of Christian fellowship.

Ours is an age when all mankind can be reached with a message. Physical facilities are making this possible as never before. It is less than a century since this first became possible, and with every decade it is becoming more feasible. If, then, Christianity possesses the answers to the persistent questions that vex the human spirit, and if these are best conveyed through a fellowship, some kind of world-wide Christian fellowship is imperative.

II

Is it true that the world-wide spread of Christianity and the embodiment of Christianity in a world-wide fellowship are essential for the emerging world society and to meet the enduring questions of men?

Most of us are suspicious of any claim of this kind made for any system. We are skeptical of proffered panaceas. We have heard so many protagonists for particular religions or for projects for social reform argue that theirs is the only road to individual or collective salvation that we are suspicious of all "world saviors." Why not a Buddhist, or a Moslem, or a Hindu, or a Confucian, or a communist world fellowship rather than one bearing the Christian name as an essential feature of the newly emerging world culture and as the means to the answers to the eternal questions of men? Or why not a combination of the various insights embodied in the several philosophies and religions of the world?

These queries are not only legitimate; they are also of primary importance. Yet to deal with them in any satisfactory manner would expand this little book far beyond the limits set by the editors. If, in their brevity, the following paragraphs seem at times dogmatic, it is purely because of lack of space and not from any desire to seek to convince by emphatic assertion.

What, then, are the reasons for advocating Christianity rather than some other religion or system as essential to the highest well-being of man in this emerging world society? Why a world-wide Christian fellowship?

1. *Because a deliberate combination of the various faiths and philosophies is not feasible, and if it were it would lack vitality.*

Between the several religions and philosophies in their basic convictions and attitudes toward the universe lie deep and wide gulfs. An honest reconciliation is impossible.

Thus, the fundamental assumption back of Buddhism is that life is not worth living. Life and suffering, so it is held, are inseparable. Since the transmigration of souls is also assumed, physical death simply means a transition to another stage of suffering. To be saved, therefore, one must be freed from life and from the endless chain of births and rebirths. One must be freed even from love, for with love for others goes suffering. This entity called "I" must be dissolved. Even the gods are subject to suffering and to birth and rebirth. Salvation is not to be found through a God, but through one's own individual efforts. I may aid my fellows (so said Buddhism at the outset) by teaching them the way of salvation, but ultimately each soul must save itself. In its later developments Buddhism experienced profound modifications of this original position. Never, however, has it fully freed itself from it.

In contrast with Buddhism, Christianity insists that life can be made worth living, that the highest goal of human existence is not the extinguishment of life, but more life, that part of the essence of this life is love, that this life is in fellowship with the eternal God, that an important aspect of salvation is the entrance upon this eternal life, and that God by an historic act in time has revealed Himself in Jesus of Nazareth and has made this salvation possible.

Islam maintains that the gulf that separates man from God is so great that God could not have a human son. A basic conviction of Christianity is, to use the words of an early Christian, that "God was in Christ reconciling the world unto himself," that in Jesus God touched human life and made it possible for men to gain authentic insight into His nature, to be transformed, and to enter into fellowship with Him.

In some of its forms Confucianism believes in Some One at the heart of the universe who has resemblances to what the Christian thinks of when he uses the word *God*. Yet Confucianism has never dreamed that God is of such a nature that through what the Christian has called the incarnation, the cross, and the resurrection, He seeks to save men from their sin and bring them into fellowship with Himself.

It need scarcely be added that, between the professed atheism of communism in its classic Marxist form and the central place given by Christianity to God who has shown Himself in Jesus a vast chasm yawns.

To be sure, between all of these systems similarities exist. Religions and philosophies, too, have borrowed extensively from one another. As a rule, however, they have taken only what is consistent with their essential nucleus and have adapted their borrowings to it. Thus, Christianity has incorporated much from rivals with which it has come in contact through the centuries.

However, those forms of Christianity that have had enough

vigor to survive and propagate themselves have not sacrificed the historic core of the faith. As a rule, too, the other faiths have held to much of their original outlook. The basic differences between religions are so great that any deliberate attempts at synthesis can result only in an anemic hybrid that lacks some of the most fundamental convictions of each and preserves merely interesting but incidental similarities. No such system—and numerous attempts have been made to create one—has ever displayed marked vitality or the ability to win widespread enthusiastic acceptance. From the very nature of the case, all such efforts are foredoomed to failure.

2. *Christianity is best fitted to form the spiritual and moral foundation of the emerging world culture because, without violence to its essence, and, indeed, as part of its fundamental nature, more than any of its rivals it combines features of the other systems that are of value for individuals and for human society and infuses them into a whole that is dominated by convictions uniquely its own.*

In its background and in the course of its formative years Christianity has had direct or indirect contact with many of the major religious and philosophic systems of mankind and has drawn from them much of what seemed to its adherents consistent with its genius. It arose out of Judaism, and the Judaism from which it came was indebted to the religions and philosophies of the Semitic peoples, Egypt, Babylonia, Persia, and Greece. In its early centuries Christianity was in touch with and incorporated elements from many religious systems in the Roman Empire—and the Roman Empire included within its broad borders more different religions than up to that time had been known in any state or country.

The ethics of the New Testament have much in common

with those of Judaism, Confucianism, Islam, and Buddhism, and, indeed, with most of the great philosophic and social systems of mankind. Yet, in their demands on men, New Testament ethics go far beyond these others. Christianity holds as the goal for the moral striving of men that they shall be perfect, even as God is perfect. This is so greatly in advance of men's present attainment that it continually draws men onward and leaves them dissatisfied short of the highest perfection. Yet, because of the love of God for men which Christianity declares to be one of the great facts of the universe, men are encouraged and not discouraged to press toward that goal.

Christianity is both this-worldly and other-worldly. At the heart of its most frequently repeated prayer it places a petition for bread. Among its tests for the character of which it declares God approves are feeding the hungry, clothing the naked, and ministering to the ill and the prisoners. From it have repeatedly emerged not only movements for alleviating the ills of those buffeted by society, but also programs for the reconstruction of society into such a form that injustice and poverty will cease. Yet Christianity also holds before men as their highest aim friendship with the invisible and eternal God and declares that its fellowship embraces not only those of its company who are now in the flesh, but also all those who through all the centuries have been in it and who have now passed beyond our present sight.

Christianity is more inclusive than other religious systems because, to a greater degree than the others, it both gives rise to vigorous action and is the inspiration of some of the outstanding mystics of the race. Indeed, some of the best-known Christian mystics have been men and women of intense activity. In Christianity the vision of God and tireless activity for the present as well as the eternal welfare of men have frequently been joined. Normally, in the Western forms of Christianity—Roman Catholicism and Protestantism—they are closely interrelated. Christians have been inspired by their faith in the God and Father of their Lord, and by their fellowship with Him, to labor for both the present and the eternal welfare of those about them. For the construction of an ideal human society, Islam has been too fatalistic and has placed too unbridgeable a gulf between man and God; Confucianism has been too this-worldly; Hinduism has been too bound to caste and too affected by the idea that this world is an illusion; Buddhism has been too other-worldly and pessimistic; Judaism is too bound to one race; and communism is too exclusively this-worldly.

3. *More than any other religion or philosophy, Christianity has shown its ability to survive the collapse of cultures with which it has been closely associated and to take root among peoples of different cultures. With each new age, indeed, Christianity has spread more widely and has displayed increased vigor and more ability to mold the cultures in the midst of which it is set. More than any other faith, therefore, it seems fitted to be permanently a part of the life of all mankind.*

Those familiar with history will at once recall that during its first five centuries Christianity became intimately associated with the Roman Empire and in time was almost identified with it and its culture. Yet it survived the death of that Empire, became the vehicle for the perpetuation of most of such Græco-Roman culture as endured, won the barbarian peoples of northern Europe, and among these peoples, particularly in northwest Europe, had more to do with shaping the cultures which next emerged than it had had in modifying the culture of the Roman Empire.

When, in the fourteenth, fifteenth, and sixteenth centuries, the culture of Medieval Europe, which Christianity had done so much to form, disintegrated, for a time Christianity seemed also to be threatened. However, it not only survived, but it also, in the Protestant and Catholic Reformations, showed fully as much vigor as ever; and in the sixteenth, seventeenth, and eighteenth centuries it spread over a wider area than had any other faith, and brought within its fold representatives from more different peoples than had ever professed any one faith. Moreover, it continued profoundly to influence culture. Witness, for instance, its extraordinary effect in incorporating benevolent idealism in the Laws of the Indies, framed for the government of the non-European subjects of Spain, the greatest colonial power of the day. Recall its part in the birth and growth of international law, and its effects through Calvinism upon Switzerland, the Netherlands, Scotland, England, and the English colonies in America.

Again, toward the close of the eighteenth century, Christianity seemed threatened. The French Revolution, the industrial revolution, the scientific method, and the Wars of Napoleon ushered in a new world. Widespread skepticism and indifference viewed Christianity as part of an outworn age. Yet in the eighteenth and nineteenth centuries Christianity experienced revivals more far-reaching than ever before, and in the nineteenth and twentieth centuries it was propagated over an even greater area than it had been in the preceding three centuries, and left a deeper impress upon human society than it had ever done before.

As samples of the revival one need mention only the many new religious orders and congregations within Roman Catholicism, the awakenings associated with the names of Wesley and Moody, the rise of the Young Men's and Young Women's Christian Associations, the Sunday-school movement, the Young People's Society for Christian Endeavor, and the student Christian movements.

As phases of the phenomenal territorial spread, one does well to recall both the achievement in the knitting of Christianity into the fabric of the new nations that arose out of the spread of European peoples in the area now occupied by the United States, Canada, Australia, New Zealand, and South Africa, and the foreign missionary movement by which Christianity was planted or nourished among non-European peoples the world around. To these and their significance we are to recur in a later chapter.

As instances of the revolutionary effect of Christianity upon nineteenth- and twentieth-century culture, the antislavery movement, the effort to regulate and even to eliminate war, and prison reform at once come to mind as having to a marked degree their historical roots in Christianity. It is highly significant that the two most influential figures of the generation which is just passing in India—Tagore and Gandhi—although neither of them would call himself Christian, have been profoundly modified by contact with Christianity, and that he who more than any other one man has shaped twentieth-century China, Sun Yat-sen, was a confessed Christian and received most of his formal education at the hands of Christian missionaries.

Now that we seem to be moving again into a new age, in many quarters Christianity is being assailed as an outworn relic of the past, an obstacle in the path of progress. In some lands the very existence of Christianity is threatened. It is the fashion even for leading Christians to bewail what they believe to be the impotence of the Church and the decay of Christian faith.

Yet the history of the past nineteen centuries contains a record of the fashion in which Christianity has broken out afresh and with enhanced power after each major age of transition. This is because there is within Christianity that which meets the continuing needs of men. It is to be expected, therefore, that this record will be repeated in the age into which we are moving and for more peoples than ever before.

4. *Its record in molding society and in meeting the needs of men warrants the belief that, better than any other religion, Christianity is fitted to become the spiritual and moral foundation of the newly emerging world culture.*

At first sight, this seems a preposterous claim. We recall the social injustices and the major defects that have spotted the history of so-called Christendom—the area in which, presumably, Christianity has had the greatest opportunity to make itself felt. We remember the exploitation of the poor by the rich that has featured all the centuries. We recall the relative impotence of the Laws of the Indies, Christian though their framers attempted to make them, to prevent the ruthless exploitation of the American Indians by the Spaniards. We have vividly in mind that it was through men from professedly Christian peoples that the African slave trade and Negro slavery became the major example of the cruel, forcible utilization of the labor of one race to enhance the wealth of another. We have seen modern industrialism with its injustices, modern huge-scale militarism, and the war which more than any other in the history of the human race affected all mankind, take their origin in Christendom.

Yet we need also to recall that the Laws of the Indies were the most notable attempt which, until then, had ever been made to ameliorate the subjugation of one race by another, that it was primarily the Christian conscience that brought an end to the Negro slave trade and to Negro slavery, that many of the attempts, proposed and actual, to make indus-trialism a blessing and not a curse trace their source to the Christian impulse, and that it is within Christendom and to a larger extent than is commonly realized by men and women who have had their consciences sharpened, their hopes quickened, and their courage strengthened by the Christian faith, that the most extensive efforts in the history of mankind have been put forth to reduce the horrors of war and eventually to eliminate war altogether. Most of the peace societies owe their inception to earnestly Christian spirits. It has been only within Christendom and chiefly from Christian individuals that international law, the Red Cross, and the League of Nations have come into being. The Institute of Pacific Relations, which is actively promot-ing better understanding among the peoples of the Pacific basin, took its rise from Christian missionaries and from those of missionary background. Much of the ethical im-pulse of communism and of some other anti-Christian radi-cal social movements is derived historically from Jewish and Christian sources. Space forbids even the mention of other movements for social amelioration and reconstruction which have had their roots in Christianity. No other religion and no remedy offered for the social ills of man has a record equal to it. Human nature being what it is, with its limi-tations of intellect and will and its proneness to sin, the achievement of Christianity has been amazing. Nowhere else on the horizon is there any other movement which, on the basis of its past record, offers so much ground for hope.

Moreover, we must always remember that the glory of Christianity is not only in its effects on groups of men, but also in what it has accomplished in the inward transforma-tion of individuals. So far as we can see, as long as men are men they are to be a mixture of physical, moral, and mental frailty, with longings for fellowship with the Eternal. They are to sin and yet to be haunted by the dream of perfection. More than any other faith, Christianity has held before men the ideal implanted in human nature, and has given men the hope and the power to struggle toward it. These quali- ties in men and in Christianity, so experience has proved, are not limited to any one range of time, or geography, or cul- ture, or race. Christianity is, therefore, uniquely equipped to become the world faith of the race.

5. *Finally, Christianity is fitted to be the inspiration and essential spiritual and moral ingredient of the new world culture because it arises out of the supreme revelation which God has made of himself to men.*

Again this must seem a dogmatic superlative, which is difficult and perhaps impossible of proof, akin to the many dogmatic claims which seek to establish their validity by the vehemence with which they are urged.

Into all the reasons for this assertion we dare not attempt to go. Many of them have been given in earlier volumes in this series. Some of them arise out of the facts given in the earlier paragraphs. That Christianity has so combined the good qualities of many faiths and yet has not been a synthetic product, that it has displayed such vitality in so many ages, peoples, and cultures, and that it has so met the persistent needs of men must arise out of correspondence with the nature of man and with the nature of the universe. These facts point to a unique connection made in Chris- tianity between the heart of the universe and the heart of man, and to a unique act of God in Jesus in making possible the transformation of men.

III

Have Christians a right to propagate their faith? More specifically, have they a right to seek to win formal adher-

ents to it? If Christianity is to be spread at all, should it not be by contagion from the lives of those who have been touched by the Christian spirit? Indeed, is it not doing wrong to the essence of Christianity consciously to seek to induce men to be Christians? Is not this a violation of the sacredness of personality, which is one of the Christian tenets?

It must at once be said that what is truly Christianity cannot be propagated by force. If the Christian faith is not accepted voluntarily, what is accepted is not really Christianity.

Yet it must also be said that the full entrance into the distinctively Christian experience is only by an act of the will or by successive acts of the will. Historically, too, Christianity has spread only through conscious effort. In part it has been accepted because men and women, hearing of it, have desired it, but back of this seemingly automatic expansion and usually associated with it has been purposeful propagation. Men seem to be so built that some kind of activity planned with that as its objective is essential to the spread of any kind of idea, whether it be a religion, the scientific method, a philosophy, or a set of social theories.

IV

Why a Christian *fellowship?* Because Christianity by its very nature brings together for friendship, for common worship, and for action in making the faith effective those who have committed themselves to it. Worship gains by fellowship. Friendships are an essential part of Christianity. Action is often most effective when by a group. Historically, a disembodied Christianity, if such there can be, is fatally truncated and has never propagated itself. To be sure, many Christians, among them some of the choicest spirits, believe that Christian missionaries should not seek to make formal converts or to gather these converts into churches. Unselfish living, they declare, is what is called for. God, so they hold, will not let it fail. Yet as a plain matter of experience, Christianity has perpetuated itself only through visible and avowedly Christian groups. Only thus can it go on from generation to generation and spread from people to people. Moreover, Christianity cannot display some of its most valuable and distinctive features unless Christians come together for worship, for fellowship, and for service.

V

Why a *world-wide* Christian fellowship? Why not content ourselves with denominations and with regional or national churches? Because it is part of the genius of Christianity to be ill content until all who profess and call themselves Christians are conscious of their common faith and are bound together by the ties of a common trust and a common faith. Because, especially, in this day when the existence of the newly emerging world culture and of civilization itself is threatened by international war, an effective, conscious, supra-national bond is desperately needed, and one that can build into this world culture a healing and unifying tie.

To realize its fullest possibilities, this world-wide Christian fellowship should embrace all men. Yet it need not wait until that far-distant day to begin to act. Again and again Christian minorities have been responsible for important modifications of the culture about them. What is needed is groups of Christians in every land bound more and more to others the world around in efforts to lift the human race to its high possibilities.

CHAPTER II

ESSENTIALS OF A WORLD-WIDE CHRISTIAN FELLOWSHIP

What must be the essential features of this world-wide Christian fellowship? Toward what goals must we strive as means of realizing it? To help us in our answer to these questions we have the character of Christianity as seen in Jesus and in the earliest followers of Jesus, the experience of Christians through nineteen centuries, the nature of man, and the kind of human society in the midst of which that fellowship must function.

1. *First of all, it must be obvious that the tie of a world-wide Christian fellowship must be the common heritage from Christ and the common experience through Him.*

All Christians, by their very name, are such because Jesus of Nazareth was born, walked the earth, taught, died, and, so his followers have claimed, was not overcome by death but ever lives. They believe in a God whom they declare they have seen in Christ and in the influences that have come from Christ. They have a common experience of a new life through Christ. It is significant that in every communion and denomination are those who bear a common likeness. In some in every church are to be seen what one of the greatest of the early Christians declared to be "the fruits of the Spirit"—love, joy, peace, long suffering, kindness, goodness, faithfulness, meekness, self-control. Organized Christianity has many divisions and at times one despairs of finding any common bond. But it is there, in this common origin and in what, with all their variations, are a common faith and a common experience.

2. *Next, it is clear that if this fellowship is to be true to the spirit of him whose name it bears, it must place its chief emphasis on love—on love for God and for one another.*

Love is the cardinal ethical precept of Christianity. Christians are enjoined to have good will toward all their neighbors, but especially toward those "of the household of faith." Love is to be the outstanding characteristic of those who have responded to the love of God. Christians are to show it especially to one another. "By this shall all men know that ye are my disciples if ye have love one for another." The only true Christian unity is that of love.

3. *Christians, if they are true to their calling, must continue to cherish the dream of a fellowship embracing all Christians.*

The dream will not down. Through the centuries Christians have been striving to make it a reality. Even after the discouragements and the failures of nineteen hundred years the hope is still there, today more potent than ever.

To be sure, *Christians have fallen far short of translating this dream into actuality.* Quarrels between Christians are the chronic punctuation of the history of the churches. One is sometimes tempted to declare that dissension has more marred the history of Christianity than it has that of any other faith.

This is largely because of human nature. All human social institutions have a record of internal strife. That is true whether they be governments, universities, families, tribes, or religious associations. Because of what they are,

men are gregarious and gather into groups for varying purposes. Because men are men, always, too, there are some
who decline to conform fully to the group. Wills clash.
The Christian emphasis on the guidance of the Spirit of
God leads some to increased dogmatism and to insistence
that their particular view of the faith has divine sanction.

Yet Christianity seeks to save men from the selfishness,
the egotism, the jealousies, and the hatreds that are ultimately the source of this strife. In this it is not without
effect. In the face of the human nature with which it has
had to deal, as we are to see in a later chapter, its successes
have been amazing.

In the light of what has just been said, although *we are
not warranted in expecting in our lifetimes a complete ful-
fillment of the dream of an all-inclusive, world-wide, perfect
Christian fellowship, we can reasonably hope to see progress
toward this end.*

4. *We must recognize the fact that most of the processes
    that Christians have traditionally used to attain this
    goal have, in practice, placed the emphasis in the
    wrong place. It is essential, therefore, that we do not
    pin to them our hope for unity.*

Christians have sought unity and fellowship through
attempting to enforce conformity to one organization or
through assent to a common creed. Organizations and
creeds have their places, and important ones, but experience has amply shown that inclusive Christian fellowship
is not to be attained through adherence either to a single
church or to one creed. The Orthodox Churches of the
Near East, though priding themselves on their loyalty to
correct intellectual statements of the faith, are sundered by
national boundaries. The Roman Catholic Church through
uniform creeds and a comprehensive organization has

brought within its fold more of those who call themselves Christians than has any other group. Yet it is far from embracing all Christians and it has been forced sadly to admit that many who are of its soul are not included in its body. Nor is there the slightest likelihood that the larger proportion of the Christians in other churches will ever seek shelter in its fold. Moreover, within Roman Catholic ranks the breaches to the only true Christian unity, that of love, have been quite as marked as between Roman Catholics and non-Roman Catholics. The internal quarrels, the jealousies, and the bitternesses between orders, between members of various nations, and between individuals run like a sinister thread through the history of this church—as of other churches.

Less and less, as time goes on, does there seem to be any likelihood of Christian unity being achieved through the adherence of all Christians to any one of the existing churches or to any one or more of the existing creeds. It is entirely outside the range of probability, for example, that the majority of Protestants will become Roman Catholics or that the Roman Catholic Church will admit Protestants on the latters' terms. Nor is there even a remote chance that the majority of Roman Catholics will become Protestant.

Neither does the merging of existing churches on the basis of compromise and equality seem to offer much promise. Most attempts of that kind have resulted in fresh organizational divisions. In spite of repeated efforts toward the formal union of churches, the number of distinct and reciprocally independent Christian churches is probably greater today than at any other time in Christian history. This is not meant to decry attempts to effect the fusion of existing bodies. Some of these have succeeded in reducing the number of existing Christian denominations and in increased strength. It is, however, meant to call attention to the fact that no world-wide fellowship inclusive of even a large majority of all Christians can be arrived at by this road.

It seems to follow, then, that a *world-wide Christian fellowship, if it is to include all Christians, or even a large majority of all Christians, is not to be achieved through the expansion of any one of the existing churches or through what is normally meant by church union. Nor is it to be attained through a federation of existing churches.* Probably it is not to be reached through any one form of organization, or, when it appears, to be expressed through any one organization. Organizations there will be, and necessarily so. They are essential to co-operation in various tasks to which Christians jointly set their hands, and to fellowship and corporate worship. Emphasis upon any single organization as the sole means to Christian unity, however, by its very nature leads to the exclusion of some who cannot conscientiously assent to the form or the full program of that organization. Moreover, it does not heal those breaches of the unity of the spirit that historically have been inseparable from organization. No, world-wide Christian fellowship is not to be achieved through one visible Church. That "blessed company of all faithful people," which is the true Church of Christ, has never taken, nor can it take, any one tangible form.

For much the same reason, *the phrase "a world Christian community" or "a world-wide Christian community," which some are now using, is probably misleading. Community* implies not only a corporate life, which in some sense must characterize a true *fellowship,* but to many has the connotation of a visible geographic location. In contrast with this, the world-wide Christian fellowship must be scattered in many lands, among many peoples, and must cut across the lines of many existing communities.

World-wide inclusive Christian fellowship is probably not to be found through the sacraments or through adherence to the final authority of the Bible.

This statement, of course, is not meant to belittle the importance either of the sacraments or of the Scriptures. Through the centuries the sacraments have been, as they are today, "a means of grace" to millions. For great numbers of Christians the Lord's Supper aids fellowship. Fortunately, too, one of the persistent characteristics of Christianity has been the prominence given to the Bible—the literary representation of the faith out of which Christianity arose and the early records of the life and sayings of Jesus and of the most prominent of the early Christians. All Christians find one of their common ties in the Bible.

Yet the Friends, among whom are undoubtedly many of the noblest Christians, do not believe in visible sacraments and cannot be brought within a world-wide Christian fellowship on that basis. The Communion, as a symbol of unity, becomes for many Christians a symbol of division, for "excommunication" has often been a means by which one body of Christians has severed fellowship with another body of Christians. Disputes over the form of baptism and over the question of whether the rite shall be administered to infants have long been a source of friction. Controversies over the interpretation of the Scriptures have been a frequent occasion for division. Although both Protestants and Roman Catholics have given prominence to the Bible, the former, in theory, although by no means always in practice, have insisted that the individual must interpret it, while the Roman Catholic has declared that the Church, through its official spokesmen, must be the authoritative interpreter.

Unless love is placed first, both the sacraments and the Bible prove as much occasions for division as for fellowship.

5. *A world-wide Christian fellowship at its best must be supra-national rather than international.*

That is to say, it must be more than a federation of national churches. One of the banes of our time is unregulated nationalism. Uncompromising sovereignty of national states is one of the greatest causes of war and one of the major threats to civilization. Christianity inevitably bears and must continue to bear the impress of the varying cultures and nations in the midst of which it is set. However, we have seen too much of the contradiction of Christianity by a church in a belligerent nation invoking the aid of God for the arms of its own state to view with equanimity a world-wide Christian fellowship made up of units in which loyalty to the nation is stronger than loyalty to the universal God and to the inclusive Christian brotherhood. The ideal must be a fellowship that transcends national lines and in which consciousness of the inclusive Christian tie is more potent than that of the nation.

6. *A world-wide Christian fellowship, if it is to deserve the name of Christian, must be both inclusive and exclusive.*

It must seek to include all who confess their primary allegiance to be to the God who has revealed Himself in Jesus. It is jeopardized if it embraces those whose primary loyalty is directed elsewhere—to another faith or to another object. For instance, a combination of the adherents of older religions, including Christianity, such as is sometimes proposed in opposition to modern irreligion, would have in it no cohesion except a common fear and would be lacking in vitality. The gulfs between the fundamental convictions of existing religions are too great to permit an enduring fellowship. Yet, in their allegiance to the God revealed in

Jesus, Christians of all names find a common ground sufficient for an enduring fellowship.

7. *However, members of the world-wide Christian fellow-
    ship must be glad of the friendship of members of
    other faiths.*

Often they must humbly acknowledge their debt to those
of other religions.   Some of us have been rebuked and
inspired by the lives of non-Christians.   In them we have
seen embodied some of the qualities which we think of as
Christian and which we know to be lacking in ourselves.
Yet, if we look at even the noblest of these souls objec-
tively and not sentimentally, we see basic differences between their attitudes and those which we feel that as Christians we should hold.   We cannot but believe that, if they
were to become Christian, certain qualities would be added
to them that would unspeakably enrich their lives.   Even
when these qualities are lacking in ourselves, they are a part
of the goal of Christian living.

8. *It must be apparent from what we have said that a world-
    wide fellowship embracing all Christians can be real-
    ized only through fresh experimentation and through
    continued, patient effort.*

It cannot come through the expansion of any existing
organization or through persistence in emphases on which
in times past most Christians have pinned their hopes for
union.   Probably no one program will prove entirely suc-
cessful.   No single avenue of approach will bring us to our
desired goal.

Some progress will be made through undertaking common tasks that do not involve discussion of ecclesiastical
organization, creeds, or sacraments.   Protestants have found
such mediums in a great variety of organizations for par-

ticular purposes that break across denominational lines. Roman Catholics and Protestants have sometimes co-operated in famine relief and have sat side by side on boards seeking to mitigate the physical distresses of men.

Frequently fellowship in worship is possible between members of different groups.

The world-wide Christian fellowship will come through the efforts of many through a variety of channels.

Always, however, we must bear in mind a fact that is too easily forgotten, that the effective bond of such a fellowship must be love—for the God who is seen in Jesus and for those who share a common allegiance to him.

9. *We must also remind ourselves again and again that the fellowship is not alone one between human beings. It is a fellowship of human beings with the "God and Father of our Lord Jesus Christ."*

The tie is not primarily the love of men for one another—although this is important—but the love of God for men. It is a fellowship in which God is the unseen partner. It is the fellowship of the "Church of Christ," a fellowship made possible because "God so loved the world that he gave his only begotten Son." It is a fellowship in which men continue to have comradeship through that "Spirit which proceedeth from the Father and the Son." In the last analysis, the hope of realizing a world-wide Christian fellowship is not the effort of men but the continuing presence of God. It is this Presence, working through and transforming imperfect men and women like ourselves, subject though we are to prejudice, jealousy, anger, and narrowness, which is at once the center of the fellowship and the ground for confidence that it can be made a reality.

CHAPTER III

RECENT STEPS TOWARD A WORLD-WIDE CHRISTIAN FELLOWSHIP

We are living in a time when, as never before, progress is being made toward the realization of a world-wide Christian fellowship. Not only is our age one that desperately needs such a fellowship. It is also one in which, as in no other, effective steps can be taken, and, indeed, are being taken, to make that fellowship a reality. This is mainly because of the extraordinary expansion of Christianity through the efforts of Christians of the past century and a quarter.

Four and a half centuries ago—a comparatively brief time in the long span of human history—Christianity was confined chiefly to the smallest of the continents: Europe. In Egypt, Western Asia, and India were Christian minorities, but these were losing ground and were on the defensive. A world-wide Christian fellowship was then an impossibility.

Even a century and a quarter ago Christianity geographically was somewhat circumscribed. To be sure, between 1500 and 1800 it had experienced a phenomenal expansion. It had been carried to the Americas and was there not only the professed faith of the white settlers, but also had been passively accepted by thousands of politically and economically subject Indians. Here and there on the coasts of Africa were small groups of Christians, most of them white traders and colonists. In India and Ceylon were a few tens of thousands of Christians, most of them in regions under the political control of Europeans. The majority of

the Filipinos had become Roman Catholics and constituted
the first Christian nation in the Far East. In the portions
of the East Indies under Dutch control a few Christian
communities had arisen. In Indo-China and China Christians numbered between two and three hundred thousand.
Korea and Japan each had a few hundreds of Christians.
Russian settlers had carried their form of Christianity across
Siberia and even into Alaska.

However, as late as 1800 any thought of a world-wide
Christian fellowship would have seemed fantastic. In much
of Western Europe, as we have suggested, Christianity was
on the defensive and was losing ground. Widespread
skepticism had chilled the enthusiasm even of many leaders
of the Church. The French Revolution and Napoleon had
uprooted much of the old order with which Christianity
had come to be closely associated, and had dealt cavalierly
with the Church. The larger part of the Americas was as
yet practically untouched by Christian folk. Christian peoples were ignorant of even the geography of most of the
interior of Africa. In India, the dominant Western authority, the English East India Company, was hostile to any
attempt to win converts to Christianity from among the
Indians. Most of Burma was inaccessible to Christian missionaries. Only minor portions of the East Indies were as
yet touched by European influence or by Christian missionaries. Christian missionaries were barred from China, and
the surviving Christian communities were declining in
numbers and morale. In Korea, persecutions were frequent. In Japan, by a series of persecutions in the seventeenth century, the government had excluded European
missionaries and believed that it had exterminated Christianity. Throughout Japan edict boards proclaimed Christianity to be an evil religion. Only in one of the southern
islands, unknown to the officials, did a few hundred Jap-

anese secretly maintain some of the rites of the faith. The islands of the Pacific, including the vast land of Australia, held practically no Christians. The great Roman Catholic missionary movement of the sixteenth and seventeenth centuries, which had been chiefly responsible for the spread of Christianity in the Americas and Asia, seemed to have spent itself. Christianity appeared to be waning.

The nineteenth and twentieth centuries have witnessed a remarkable change. The religious revivals of which we spoke in an earlier chapter brought to Christianity a greater vigor than it had yet known. A missionary movement arose unequalled in the history not only of Christianity, but also of any other faith. Never before had any set of ideas, religious or secular, been propagated over so wide an area by so many professional agents supported by the voluntary gifts of so many millions of people.

In the United States, thanks very largely to this missionary movement, the pioneers were followed on the westward-moving frontier. The immigrants from Europe were accompanied as they settled in field and city, churches were built for them, and a clergy trained. The emancipated Negro was brought into the Church and was assisted through schools to progress toward the social, intellectual, economic, and spiritual equality to which political action had theoretically opened the door. So well was the work of the missionary accomplished that in 1937 not only had the actual number of Christians within the United States vastly increased, but the proportion of the population who claimed church membership had more than doubled.

In Canada, Australia, New Zealand, and in the Argentine and Uruguay, new nations of European stock emerged, which, through the active efforts of Christians, possessed strong branches of the Church.

This building of Christianity into the texture of the new

nations of white stock did not come about automatically. It was the result of deliberate and persistent action on the part of hundreds of thousands. Nor was it planned or directed by any one central bureau or by a master mind. It was the outgrowth of the prodigious vitality of the Christianity of the period. It was not confined to one wing of Christianity. Indeed, those branches of Christianity that did not have a share in it were comparatively few. In the United States, the most populous of the new nations, Christianity was more variegated than it had ever been in any one land, and this was largely because so many forms of the faith were represented among the immigrants and succeeded in holding the latter to their ancestral churches.

Christianity has continued to be strongest numerically among peoples of European descent, but it has been planted among the large majority of other peoples and cultures. Indeed, it is only among a few score of smaller tribes of primitive culture that it is not present. Wherever it has gone it has not only won adherents, it has also worked marked transformation in the lives of individuals and of groups. The nineteenth and twentieth centuries have been a period when non-European cultures have been profoundly modified under the impact of European peoples. In this process Christian missionaries have thrown the weight of their efforts toward making that impact a blessing and not a curse. They have led the way in introducing constructive features of Western culture—notably education, medicine, and improvements in agriculture.

Among most of the tribes of American Indians there are Christians. Indeed, the large majority of the members of the native races of the Americas are now professing Christians. Many of these are the descendants of pre-nineteenth-century converts. Many others, however, are the results of the missions of the past century and a quarter. In both

North and South America, hundreds of missionaries are even now giving their lives in the service of the Indians. Schools, churches, and increasing Indian Christian communities attest their presence and their devotion.

The second half of the nineteenth century witnessed the opening of the interior of Africa by the white man and the political partition of the continent among European governments. The twentieth century is seeing the disintegration of the cultures of Negro Africa under the impact of Western culture. In this white penetration of Africa, Christian missionaries have had an important part. Frequently they have been pioneers. They have helped to destroy most of the old. They have, however, also led in assisting the Negro to make his adjustment to the new in a way that will be helpful to him. It is they who are reducing the tongues of Negro Africa to writing, are creating the beginnings of a literature in them, and are conducting most of the schools by which the African is being prepared to take his place in the world so suddenly thrust upon him. In many areas missionaries are providing most or all of the medical service. In the great mining areas of South Africa they are putting forth valiant efforts to keep the African from deteriorating through intimate contact with the white man's industrial civilization. Wherever he has gone, the missionary is calling into existence Christian groups and is training Africans to lead them.

In North Africa, including Egypt, in Western Asia, and in Persia, Christian missionaries have faced some of their most perplexing problems. Traditionally, Moslems have been very difficult to win to the Christian faith. The law of Islam against apostasy is stringent. Under Moslem governments baptism has frequently meant death. As a result, the extensive Christian missions from western Europe and the United States have had their chief tangible successes among the older churches. Thousands from these bodies have become affiliated with the Roman Catholic Church. Others in considerable numbers have formed themselves into groups that are essentially Protestant in character. However, real if less tangible results have followed among Moslems. A few Moslems have formally announced themselves as converts. Particularly in Persia—or, to give that land its present official name, Iran—there is a beginning of a movement of Moslems into the Christian churches. More widespread has been the effect of Christian schools and hospitals and of other philanthropic enterprises, such as Near East Relief. By precept and example these agencies have disseminated ideals of private living and of social relations that historically have their source in Christianity. The weakness lies in the lack of Christian groups drawn from former Moslems to perpetuate these ideals.

In India is one of the largest aggregations of mankind. Here live between three hundred and fifty and three hundred and seventy-five millions, and the increase is at the rate of about two and a half millions a year. Racially, linguistically, and religiously more varied than western Europe, in the past century, for the first time in its history, India has all been brought under one political rule, that of the British. Today the rising tide of nationalism gives assurance of a large degree of home rule and even threatens to sweep the land out of the British Empire.

Within India Christian missionaries have long been present. The ancient communities of Syrian Christians go back to so early a date that we do not know precisely how they were founded. Roman Catholics have been at work continuously since the close of the fifteenth century, and Protestants since the first half of the eighteenth century. Roman Catholic and Protestant missionaries are from a number of nations, and Protestants from many different denominations. As a consequence, the Christians of India number about six millions and are increasing proportionately more rapidly than is the population of the land as a whole. Among them are represented many of the historic branches of Christianity. The result is present division but the future possibility of the richness of fellowship that comes from a diversity of traditions.

The large majority of the Christians of India, particularly of the Protestants, are from the depressed classes. The depressed classes, or outcastes, are the underprivileged of the land. By the accident of birth they are condemned to poverty, to the performance of the menial tasks of the community, to social obloquy, and, frequently, to moral and spiritual degradation. To them Christianity has opened a door of hope—self-respect, education, and spiritual and moral improvement. For instance, thanks to mission schools and in spite of the fact that the overwhelming majority of Protestant Christians are from the outcastes, the percentage of Protestant Christians who are literate is three times that of the total population.

For women, too, Christianity has meant enlarged opportunity. Again as an example, the percentage of women in the Protestant churches who can read and write is ten times that of the women of the nation as a whole.

It is not only among the depressed classes and the women that Christianity has penetrated India. It has also profoundly affected the entire nation. Partly because the ties of caste and family are strong and stand in the way, formal conversions from the upper classes, though by no means lacking, are comparatively few. Yet the educated especially have felt the effect of Christianity. Through Christian schools and through the study of English literature, which is one of the features of British education in India, numbers have adopted much from Christian ideals in ethics and religion.   There are said to be many "invisible Christians," who have not affiliated themselves with any church.   It is, however, extremely unlikely that through such individuals, noble though many of them are in character, Christianity will continue in India as a growing power.   Only through visible, confessedly Christian fellowships can Christianity be perpetuated.

In Ceylon, Roman Catholic Christians have long been numerous.   Protestantism is also represented, but by smaller numbers.

In Burma, Christianity has made but little progress among the Burmese proper, but it has experienced phenomenal gains among tribes of more nearly primitive culture.   Particularly has it transformed the Karens and led them into the beginnings of a wholesome community life.

In Siam, the number of Christians is small, but Christian schools are having a marked effect upon the land.

In French Indo-China, very few Protestant missionaries have ever labored.   Roman Catholic missionaries are numerous and there is a large and steadily growing body of Roman Catholic Christians.

The native stocks of the Malay Peninsula are predominantly Moslem, and, as a result, few from among them have become Christians.   However, Chinese have come to the region, and of these a good many are now Christians.

The Dutch East Indies have been and are the scene of a remarkable growth of Christian communities.   Here, for generations, Dutch and German missionaries have been at work.   In a few of the smaller islands Christians are in the majority.   In some instances, notably among the Bataks of Sumatra, remarkable transformations have been wrought in the lives of entire peoples.   Java contains more than half the population of the archipelago.   Since it is predominantly Moslem in religion and since Islam offers stubborn resistance to any other faith, the number of Christians from the older Javanese stocks is small. However, even here and from among Moslems some converts have been won.

At the outset of the nineteenth century, as we have seen, the Philippine Islands were predominantly Christian in name. They are so today. In the course of the past century and a quarter still more of the remaining animistic tribes have become Christian. Since the American occupation, in 1898, Protestantism has entered and, partly because of the competition that it has offered, the quality of the Roman Catholicism of the islands has improved.

The islands of the Pacific were the scene of some of the most spectacular of the missionary successes of the nineteenth century. Here are hundreds of islands, most of them small. In 1800 the populations were animistic in faith and primitive in culture. Missionaries, chiefly Protestants, first entered in the seventeen nineties. In island group after island group, after an initial period of resistance and persecution, the majority of the population became Christian. A reconstruction of the entire life of the people was called for if that life were to be Christian. This the missionary undertook.

This was the more imperative because repeatedly the missionaries arrived before European governments had extended their colonial administration over the islands and because the native peoples were threatened not only by their indigenous vices, but also by exploitation by white traders, by the accentuation of tribal wars through the introduction of firearms, and by the vices and diseases of the white man.

The missionary proved of incalculable value. Sometimes he made serious mistakes. An occasional missionary succumbed to the temptations of his environment. However, the story overwhelmingly redounds to the credit of

Christianity. By schools and by becoming the channel of fresh spiritual and moral forces, the missionary aided these "children of nature" in making the transition to the white man's world with less pain and disaster than would other-wise have been theirs. Because of economic and political pressure from Europe and America, the collapse of the old native societies was inevitable. The missionary has helped to make the new better than it would otherwise have been. On many of the islands Christian communities have arisen, which have been wholesome for the local populations and from which "native" missionaries have gone out in heroic fashion to other islands, some of them thousands of miles distant.

China has been a major center of nineteenth and twen-tieth century missions. Here at times have been more mis-sionaries than in any other one country. The increase came particularly after 1900. Until the closing decade of the nineteenth century, the Chinese stubbornly resisted the influx of Occidental culture. Their change of mind was brought about by their defeat, in 1894-1895, by a West-ernized Japan, by their humiliation at the hands of the great powers in 1900 and 1901 through the suppression of the Boxer outbreak, and by their feeling of helplessness, in 1904-1905, while Russia and Japan fought each other on Chinese soil. The Chinese thereupon set about the process of recon-structing their national life. To preserve their badly threatened political independence, they decided to sacri-fice their proudly guarded cultural independence. The result was a cultural revolution, which, for its thorough-going character and for the large number of people involved, is unequalled in the history of the world. The Christian forces of the Occident saw in this transformation a chal-lenge. It has been and still is an opportunity to help the Chinese in every wholesome manner possible in the travail of their transition and to build Christianity into the structure of the new national life.

In a great variety of ways Christian missionaries have sought to serve the changing China. They have pioneered in the introduction of modern medicine. The modern medical profession and public-health programs of China are being built on foundations laid by them. They have led the way in building modern schools. Today the Chinese are conducting their own modern schools, but in secondary and higher education Christian schools of missionary origin still have an important place. Missionaries introduced methods for teaching the blind to read. They founded the first asylum for the insane. They have fought the opium traffic. They have led the way in new methods of famine relief. In an effort to prevent famine and to improve the physical standard of living, they have pioneered in the introduction of Western methods of forestry and agriculture.

Through preaching and through the preparation and distribution of literature, notably of translations of the Bible, missionaries have spread broadcast in China something of a knowledge of the Christian message. Out of these efforts and through personal contacts missionaries have given rise to Christian communities, most of them small, which can be continuing centers of Christian influence in the life of China. The number of professed Christians in China today is not far from four millions. Of these, about three millions are Roman Catholics and something less than a million Protestants. Roman Catholicism is stronger at least partly because it has been continuously in China nearly three times longer than has Protestant Christianity.

It is important and significant, however, that Protestantism is making a much deeper impression upon the culture of China as a whole than is Roman Catholicism. This is true in education and medicine and in most philanthropic enterprises. Of the Christians who are exerting a marked influence on the nation, practically all are Protestants. Protestantism is having an effect far out of proportion to its numerical strength. So far as present conditions warrant a prophecy, if Christianity is to continue to mold China as a whole, it will have to be chiefly through the successors of Protestant Christian communities, which now number only about one fourth of one per cent of the total population.

In most of the regions that were once dependencies of the Chinese Empire and which China still counts as technically part of her domains, Christianity is but slightly represented. Tibet is geographically inaccessible and religiously and politically under the control of Lamaistic Buddhism. Only a few Christian missionaries labor for the Tibetans, and these only on the borders. In Chinese Turkestan (Sinkiang), a large territory, missionaries are not numerous. Outer Mongolia has had very few. Inner Mongolia, into which many Chinese have moved, and which the Chinese Government has organized into provinces, has more. In Manchukuo, the former Manchuria, the population is predominantly Chinese. Here are some strong missions, both Protestant and Roman Catholic.

Korea, now a part of the Japanese Empire, until 1910 preserved some features of its former independence. Roman Catholicism has been in the land since the close of the eighteenth century, although until the last quarter of the nineteenth century it was subject to repeated and violent persecutions. Protestantism has been present only for a little over fifty years. Today Protestantism is stronger than Roman Catholicism. Its missionaries are chiefly from the United States. As in China, it has had an important place in pioneering in modern education and medicine. The Protestant congregations are, as a rule, independent of any foreign financial aid, and the Korean Christians have shown great zeal in propagating their faith.

In Japan proper, as in Korea, Protestant Christians out-number Roman Catholics and are chiefly the fruits of missions from the United States. In sharp contrast with India, Christians are mainly from the urban middle classes and scarcely at all from the rural population and the less privileged elements. Reflecting the national pride of Japan, the Protestant churches are for the most part quite independent of any foreign control or financial assistance. Japan is almost the only land outside of Russia in which a mission of the Russian Orthodox Church has made converts from among non-Russians.

Although in Japan Christians of all groups number less than one half of one per cent of the population, their proportionate growth is more rapid than that of the population as a whole, and Christianity is having an influence far out of proportion to its numerical strength. Buddhism and the native Shinto sects bear marks of contact with it. Buddhism has paid Christianity the sincere flattery of adopting many of the latter's methods of social service and religious education. Movements for international outlook in contrast with the intense nationalism of the land are deeply indebted to Christianity. Many humanitarian enterprises, especially for the underprivileged and for the elimination of certain social ills, are under obligation to it for their inception and leadership. The Christmas festival has become popular, and although for the majority it probably has no more religious significance than for multitudes in what is traditionally termed Christendom, something of its true import cannot fail to come to many.

In very few lands, then, is Christianity unrepresented. In a few, such as Afghanistan and most of Tibet, no missionaries are resident. In some lands, severe losses have been experienced. In Mexico Christianity has suffered a partial reverse. In Germany it is fighting for its life. In Turkey and the U. S. S. R. no active propagation of Christianity is permitted. In the U. S. S. R. a campaign against Christianity, as against all historic religion, is persistently waged, and the Church has distinctly lost ground. Yet in Mexico Christianity is far from dead, in Germany it is displaying remarkable vitality, and in both Turkey and the U. S. S. R. the Church continues and Christian services are regularly held. In Turkey, too, Christian missionaries still reside, although their activities are restricted to the teaching of secular subjects and to medical and various forms of social service.

It is a stirring record, this world-wide spread of Christianity in the past century and a quarter. The amount of devotion that has gone into it and still goes into it and the effects upon individuals and upon the collective life of whole tribes and nations are amazing.

The progress of Christianity cannot be measured by accessions to the churches, although these are impressive. It is seen, rather, in the transformation of individual lives and in the permeation and the wholesome modifications of whole peoples and cultures. Some of the groups whose collective life has been altered for good are primitive tribes in Africa, in the islands of the Pacific, and in the hills and mountains of Asia. Others are nations of advanced cultures who number their populations by the millions. Here is a movement that has operated unspectacularly and that has often been misunderstood and maligned, but whose effects have been seen in every quarter of the globe and among many peoples have been prodigious. The Christian missionary enterprise has been one of the greatest beneficent movements of the ages.

What progress, if any, has been made toward knitting the many Christian communities established by this enterprise together with Christian communities that antedate the nineteenth century, into a world-wide fellowship? One of the characteristics of nineteenth- and twentieth-century missions has been the diversity of agencies through which it has been carried on. In this is one of the evidences of the abounding vitality of the movement. Missions have not been the work of any one branch of Christianity. Denominationally they have resulted in a Joseph's coat of many colors. Christianity is today more multiform than ever before. What, if anything, has been done to draw into a conscious fellowship the adherents of this extraordinarily diverse Christianity?

Again the record has been amazing and most encouraging to those who dream of such a fellowship.

In the first place in geographic extent and in numerical strength is the Roman Catholic Church. No other one institution that the human race has ever seen has equalled it in the numbers of countries and peoples among which it is found. Organizationally the tie that holds it together is today stronger than at any previous time. The Roman Catholic Church is not so much weakened by sectionalism and local feeling as in the Roman Empire and in the Middle Ages and is not so much under the control of the governments of strong nation states as from the fifteenth into the nineteenth century. To be sure, national rivalries and the jealousies between religious orders and leading ecclesiastics still exist. The outward façade of unity, so imposing and comprehensive, does not insure that inward and less tangible unity of love which is essential to true Christian fellowship. Yet it does help to make possible a consciousness of fellowship among many of the millions who are communicants of the Roman Catholic Church.

In the next place, Protestantism has made striking progress toward an inclusive fellowship within its own ranks. In some respects this is more difficult for Protestantism than for Roman Catholicism. By its very nature Protestantism tends to endless organizational divisions. The emphasis upon the obligation of the individual to think for himself, upon the duty of private judgment, tends toward individualism and the emergence of many sects. Two seemingly contradictory movements are apparent in Protestantism today. On the one hand, the number of sects has never been so large, and it increases each year. On the other hand, never have the Christians of the Protestant tradition approached so nearly to solidarity of spirit and never have they been bound together by so many ties that cut across national and denominational boundaries.

Of these inclusive ties we can take time to mention only a few. A complete catalogue would fill a volume. One of the tendencies of Protestantism, especially in its early days, has been to be organized into national churches. Today a number of the denominations have forms of fellowship that transcend national boundaries. This has been true not only of the Baptists and Disciples of Christ, who have never been a state church, but also of some of the communions, notably the Anglicans and the Lutherans, who have traditionally been organized as state churches. In some instances the actual union of existing denominations has occurred—such as the United Church of Canada, the Church of Christ in China, the South India United Church, the Congregational-Christian fusion in the United States, the union of a number of the Methodist bodies in Great Britain, and the reunion between the Church of Scotland and the Free Church of Scotland. Often there are formal federations that do not sacrifice the autonomy of denominational units —such as the Federal Council of Churches of Christ in the United States and various city councils of churches. In more instances members of various denominations have come together in organizations for particular purposes. The Young Men's and Young Women's Christian Associations, the Young People's Societies of Christian Endeavor, the World's Sunday School Association, the World's Student Christian Federation, the World Conference on Faith and Order, and the Universal Christian Council for Life and Work are well-known examples of groupings that cut across both denominational and national lines and which are world-wide in their scope. Even now steps are being taken to bring into existence a World Council of Churches, which is designed to include not only churches of the Protestant tradition, but also the Eastern Churches.

Most inclusive of all the organizations of Protestants that are now actually in existence is one that has arisen out of the foreign missionary enterprise—the International Missionary Council. This is made up of delegates from various national and regional bodies, which in their turn are composed of representatives of denominational bodies—such as the National Christian Council of India, the National Christian Council of Japan, the Foreign Missions Conference of North America, the Conference of Missionary Societies in Great Britain and Ireland, the National Christian Council of the Philippines, and the Near East Christian Council. Based in large part upon official ecclesiastical organizations, and, in the case of the international and the larger national units, with salaried secretariats, the International Missionary Council and its constituent bodies are unique in the history of Christianity as formal ties and channels for fellowship among those of the Protestant tradition. They are gifts of the missionary enterprise to a world-wide Christian fellowship. Although, as we have suggested, that fellowship is not to be identified with any one organization and is probably not to be achieved through one visible body, for Protestantism the International Missionary Council is the most nearly inclusive visible bond that has thus far been developed.

As between the major historic divisions of Christianity —Roman Catholic, Protestant, and the various Eastern Churches—the record of fellowship is not so encouraging. Between these communions the gulfs are deep and are hedged about by century-long prejudices and by reciprocal anathemas. Yet these gulfs are by no means fathomless or unbridgeable. Underneath them is the foundation of a common origin, a common body of sacred writings, and a common loyalty to Christ. Increasingly, attempts are being made, not to obliterate them, but to facilitate friendly intercourse across them. Many of these attempts take the form of personal friendships. Some are organizational. Thus, the World Conference on Faith and Order draws together members from various Eastern Churches and of most of the major Protestant bodies for the friendly discussion of agreements and differences. Some from the Eastern Churches attended the Conference on Church, State, and Society in 1937. The Fellowship of St. Sergius and St. Albans brings together, for fellowship in worship and discussion, members of the Anglican and Russian Orthodox Churches. In some of the units of the Young Men's and Young Women's Christian Associations, Roman Catholics and Protestants and Protestants and Orthodox join in common action. In several of the conferences held under the World's Student Christian Federation and of its units Roman Catholic, Orthodox, and Protestant have mingled, not as official delegates, but as individuals. In the United States, through the efforts of one organization, Protestants, Roman Catholics, and Jews have spoken from the same platforms in an effort at amicable understanding. In various ways there is emerging before our eyes a fellowship that does not seek to do violence to individual convictions, but to bring richness through diversity.

CHAPTER IV

PROBLEMS STILL TO BE SOLVED

It is so obvious as to be a banality that the world-wide Christian fellowship is not yet a reality. In spite of the remarkable progress that the past century and a quarter have witnessed, we cannot speak of it as being a present fact.

The problems still to be solved are many.

1. *First of all, we must remind ourselves of the numerical weakness of the so-called younger churches.*

In spite of its remarkable expansion of the past four centuries, Christianity is still chiefly the faith of Occidental peoples. In Negro Africa, Christians number only about 2 or 3 per cent of the population. In India, they are less than 2 per cent. In China, they are under 1 per cent, and in Japan, only about 0.5 per cent of the total population. In each of these areas and nations they are, to be sure, increasing fairly steadily and rapidly, but at least in India and Japan, where census figures are reasonably exact, more are added to the population each year than come into the Christian faith. Numerically, these younger churches are still very feeble.

2. *In several lands the opposition to Christianity has recently become particularly acute.*

In the vast land of the U. S. S. R., Christianity is on the defensive and seems to be retreating. The same is true in Turkey. In each of these lands ample reasons exist for criticism of the churches that are there the most prominent representatives of Christianity. The opposition to them is quite

understandable. Yet whatever the reasons, in the U. S. S. R.
and Turkey Christianity has been losing ground. So, too,
as we have suggested, in some other lands, notably in Germany and Mexico, Christianity is fighting with its back to
the wall. In Japan, hyper-nationalists look upon it with
suspicion as too international. It is less than ten years since
in China an anti-religious movement brought a halt for a
time to the growth of the Church. Nationalism, united with
systems of thought, such as communism, fascism, and national socialism, often views Christianity as an enemy. For
many millions the secular attitude toward life undercuts
the enthusiasm for a faith such as Christianity, which claims
the sanction of what is usually termed the supernatural and
is not only this-worldly, but also other-worldly.

Incidentally, it may be remarked that these threats are
usually best countered indirectly and not by a frontal at-
tack. In lands where the Church has traditionally been
strong, but obscurantist, accusations can better be met by
removing the abuses and awaking the Church from its
lethargy than by vituperation of the critics. In some lands
Christians must expect undeserved persecution. Christian
principles run counter to the official ethics and the nationalist program. Yet even here Christians can scarcely be true
to their ideals if they bring a railing accusation against their
opponents. They must prove by the evidence of their lives
the worth of their faith.

3. *As we have suggested, the organizational cleavages among
    Christians seem to be growing not less but more
    numerous.*

Most of the historic divisions continue. To these are
added fresh sects, many of them on the newer geographic
frontiers of Christianity.

It need scarcely be said that denominations and churches must not be denounced out of hand as enemies of Christianity. To be sure, some of them have arisen through envy and strife, from the selfish ambitions and narrow dogmatisms of vigorous men. On the other hand, the larger and more persistent ones possess special emphases and traditions that have contributions to make to the entire Christian fellowship. However, the multiplication of denominations makes more difficult a world-wide Christian fellowship.

In spite of the present trend toward an inclusive fellowship and even the formal union of varying ecclesiastical bodies, new divisions continue to appear. Thus, in South Africa many new sects are emerging among the Bantu Christians. The younger churches planted by nineteenth- and twentieth-century missions, especially those of the Protestant tradition, will almost inevitably, as they become rooted in the soil, tend to separate and to re-group themselves according to inherited backgrounds and the convictions of outstanding leaders.

The main divisions of organized Christianity show no signs of being obliterated. Friendships are being developed across the barriers that divide Roman Catholic from Protestant and Protestant from Orthodox. However, there is no likelihood that within a century or even three or four centuries these streams will merge, or that one stream will be augmented by the others becoming tributary to it and pouring their waters into it.

Even within Protestantism many and perhaps most of the larger denominations and national churches appear vigorous and seem headed for longevity. Tradition, inertia, and hereditary loyalties alone insure a continued existence. Added to these are convictions centering about distinctive tenets.

4. National and racial cleavages give no indication of disappearing.

For instance, any thought of an early merger of the Church of England and the Church of Scotland is fantastic. Both bodies are too deeply rooted in national affections, in distinct traditions, and in sincerely held and incompatible convictions to permit of that. Even in bodies of a common theological tradition, national lines prevent union. Thus, a formal fusion of the various Lutheran bodies is highly unlikely. Nor are the Reformed Churches of Hungary, Scotland, the Netherlands, Switzerland, and France, although having a common Calvinistic heritage, at all likely to come together in one closely knit ecclesiastical structure. It is difficult, although, fortunately, proved by experience not to be impossible, for Japanese and Chinese Christians, even of the same denominations, to enjoy fellowship unbroken by the tension between the two nations. The differences that sever various of the ancient Eastern Churches —Copts, Armenians, Jacobites, Assyrians (Nestorians), and Greeks—are as much national and racial as they are creedal. In the United States, Negro denominations exist; in hundreds of communities separate Negro and white congregations are found; and across the racial gulf fellowship is usually scanty or entirely absent.

Organizational unity does not always effectively overcome these obstacles. Witness the manner in which French and German Roman Catholics slew each other in the late World War.

5. In addition to national and racial divisions, there are social cleavages.

In England the distinction between members of the Established Church and of the various Non-Conformist bodies tends to follow class lines. Any one familiar with the denominational complexion of the United States or with any city or town in the United States is quite aware that the distinctions between denominations and between the various churches in a local community are fully as much social as organizational and creedal.

6. *Always, moreover, the dream of fellowship encounters obstacles inherent in man as man.*

As human beings we are strange contradictions. We are gregarious creatures who tend toward fellowship. We have capacities for heroism, for a sacrificial love that forgets itself in the service of others, and for the adoration of the God of love. The majority of Christians have insisted through the centuries that Jesus, who gave himself in loving service in the cities and villages of Galilee and Judea and who went voluntarily to the cross, was fully man as well as the unique revelation of God. Yet as a seemingly integral part of human nature, envy, faction, striving for self-aggrandizement, hatred, bitterness, the desire for revenge, and many another trait actively oppose what the Christian means by fellowship.

These unlovely and anti-social features of the human spirit are not at once removed by a dedication of the self to God. In relatively few do they ever completely disappear. Christians are "being saved" from them, as the experience of thousands shows, but very few are fully freed from them. They rise, and will continue to rise, to plague efforts at fellowship, not only on a world-wide scale and between existing ecclesiastical bodies, but also within existing bodies. They are never more evident than within local congregations and even within families.

7. *Still to be solved in any adequate fashion, moreover, is the problem of making Christianity effective in meeting staggering needs of world dimensions.*

As we have suggested, Christianity has profoundly influenced national and regional cultures, not only where it has been longest represented by numerically strong churches, in the Occident, but also in lands where it has more recently come in force and where it is numerically still weak, as in China and in much of Negro Africa. Moreover, in the group of peoples that was once known as Christendom it has helped to mold the collective life, as in international law and in several humanitarian movements.

However, never even within Christendom has Christianity been able to make its ideals dominant. They have been in conflict with other and quite contrary traditions and purposes.

Now that the external framework of a world-wide culture is emerging, and is embracing lands in which Christian communities are still relatively weak, in the total stream of civilization Christianity is, at least for the time, much more diluted than it has been in the West at any time since the days of the Emperor Constantine. As we have earlier suggested, the features thus far common to the nascent world culture are the increased knowledge and mastery of man's physical environment and the scientific procedures by which these have been made possible. In the realm of ideals there is little or no common ground and increased conflict is the order of the day.

To the resolving of these conflicts and to the solution of some of the problems that underlie them, Christians the world around must begin addressing themselves. The threat of war, class and race conflicts, economic inequalities that enter as a cause into several of the strains, in many lands the problem of subsistence—these and others akin to them clamor for attention if the present forms taken by the drift toward a world culture are not to bring disaster to great sections of the human race.

Christians cannot hope alone and unaided to solve these problems. Numerically they are still too weak, particularly in some of the larger masses of population, to do that. Nor is it reasonable to hope that in the near future even a large minority of Christians will unite on any one program for their solution. There is no detailed blueprint of a Christian world order. In the nature of the case, there cannot be. It is, however, not too much to hope that the world over many Christians, as Christians, will address themselves to these and like issues. Indeed, in seeking so to address themselves, they may make significant contributions toward bringing the world-wide Christian fellowship out of the realms of dreams into actuality.

CHAPTER V

NEXT STEPS

What are the next steps toward making a world-wide Christian fellowship more of a reality? In the light of the nature of the problems and of the obstacles, what is feasible? In what directions can efforts be put forth with some reasonable hope that they will lead toward the desired goal? If such action is possible, it is obviously imperative.

1. *It is clear that the "younger churches" must be substantially strengthened numerically.*

Particularly among great peoples such as the Chinese, the Japanese, and the Indians, Christians are still far too few permanently to exercise much influence. The surprising effect that they are now having on these peoples is due in part to the nature of Christianity, but it is also due to circumstances that in their very nature are transitory.

Christians, both native born and foreign missionaries, owe their position largely to their function as pioneers of certain phases of Western culture. To most non-Occidental peoples, Western culture was introduced chiefly by merchants, soldiers, and diplomats. The primary cause of the expansion of European peoples has been economic—the desire for markets and raw materials. Had never a Christian missionary put his foot on the gang-plank of a trans-oceanic ship the transformation of the cultures of non-European peoples would have taken place about when it did and would have been fully as revolutionary as it has proved to be. Without the missionary, however, the resulting cultures would have been very different. What the missionary has done has been to introduce a dynamic that has better enabled non-European peoples to make of the transition a blessing and not a curse, and to lead the way in the introduction of certain phases of Western culture that without him would not have come so quickly and in some places might not have come at all. As we have seen, in modern education and medicine, in scientific methods of forestry and agriculture, and in several types of humanitarian endeavor, missionaries have blazed new trails. It is in no small degree because they were pioneers in methods that non-European peoples eventually found highly desirable that missionaries and Christians trained by them have had such a part in shaping the lives of non-European peoples and that Christians have had an influence all out of proportion to their numbers. It has been very fortunate for non-European peoples that Christian missionaries have been at hand to render this service. Here, indeed, has been one of the outstanding contributions of Christianity to the movements of the nineteenth and twentieth centuries.

That condition, however, is temporary. As non-European peoples adjust themselves to the Occident and take their place in the world culture, men from their own ranks, non-Christian as well as Christian, assume the leadership under the new conditions as they did under the old. Such of science and education as enters from the West comes increasingly through secular channels. Christianity must more and more make its way through other mediums than schools, hospitals, gymnasiums, and famine relief. It must depend less and less upon foreigners—although these still have a place—and more and more upon native-born Christians.

If, under these new circumstances, Christianity is to continue to increase in influence, the numbers of its adherents in the "lands of the younger churches" must multiply. If the "younger churches" are not strengthened, they will in time tend to become small, self-centered minorities, on the defensive against absorption, holding themselves aloof from the community as a whole and having but very little effect upon the life of the nation. In such a case, theirs may be a fate similar to that of the Moslems in China, the Parsees (Zoroastrians) in India, the Coptic Christians in Egypt, and the Jacobite Christians in Syria—each of them a minority preserving its own faith and customs, but making few converts and affecting its surroundings but little.

The strengthening of the "younger churches" must, of course, be more than a matter of numbers. Quality must be maintained and improved. Christianity spreads not alone through an increase in the census strength of its adherents, but also and chiefly from the quality of life that radiates from those who bear that name. A small group of devoted, intelligently earnest Christians may have a more striking effect on an entire people than a much larger body whose Christian profession is superficial. Yet there must also be numbers.

2. *What we have usually called "foreign missions" must be continued and re-enforced.*

This is partly because of the necessity, just mentioned, of strengthening the "younger churches." It is also because of the need of all men everywhere for the Christian Gospel. Since the "younger churches" are numerically too weak to reach all in the nations in which they are set, for at least a generation to come they will require assistance from the older churches in personnel and perhaps in money. Moreover, in some lands, as in Persia, Tibet, Chinese Turkestan, and Outer Mongolia, Christians are so few that a "younger church," rooted in the soil, can scarcely be said to exist. The same is true of many tribes in India, of the back districts of China, of Burma, of Africa, and of some of the East Indies. Here the foreign missionary must for years to come carry the main part of the burden of representing the Christian faith and of transmitting the Christian message.

The foreign missionary enterprise must not be discontinued, as some would have us believe, but augmented. This is an absolutely essential feature of a wise Christian statesmanship that plans with the world in mind and in the hope of having in every major land a Christian element strong enough to mold the newly emerging world culture. Without the missionary enterprise, any talk of a world-wide Christian fellowship or of even a partially Christian world order must be quite futile.

Foreign missions demand the ablest and the finest-spirited men and women of the older churches. No more challenging calling exists. The problems to be dealt with are so difficult and exacting that the highest standards of mind and heart are required of those who are chosen for the task. The necessity of making oneself sympathetically and understandingly at home in an alien culture and among an alien people, the tact, the faith, and the devotion required to deal with prejudice, to make the needed adjustments in methods, to win friendships, and to persevere in the face of discouragements, and the intelligence demanded to meet strange problems, call for the finest that the older churches can give. The best is none too good for foreign missionary staffs.

3. *Christian foreign missions must not only be continued and strengthened; they must also be modified and in some areas be radically altered.*

This is not because they have failed. It is because the environment in the midst of which they work is being revolutionized. Just because they have, in general, been so admirably adapted to particular conditions, with the changing of their setting they also must be made over.

Not every method nor all phases of current programs

should be abandoned. In many areas situations for which existing missionary procedures have been designed still persist. Moreover, some of the greatest needs of men are of the continuing kind and are to be met in much the same way from age to age.

One of the innovations required is an increased emphasis upon on-going Christian communities. The word *church* might be used in place of *community,* and, if one interprets it broadly enough, is probably to be preferred. *Community* is employed because the organizational expressions of Christian fellowship may in some lands prove to be very different from those which we have known in the Occident and which we have been accustomed to associate with *church.* If Christianity is to persist, it must be through visible, on-going communities. At least this has been the experience of the past and it is hard to see how in any future age it will be otherwise.

In theory, both Roman Catholic and Protestant missionaries have stressed the building of the Church. In practice, Roman Catholics have lived up to their theory. In contrast, Protestant missionaries have by no means always done so. They have seen so many desperate immediate human needs that, feeling that as Christians they could not turn aside from them, they have striven to meet them. A large proportion of their energy has gone into schools, hospitals, famine relief, improved methods of agriculture and forestry, and many another humanitarian enterprise. They have hoped, of course, that through these multiform contacts and expressions of the Christian spirit many would be led to become Christians and into membership in the Church. In giving themselves to these tasks, Protestant missionaries have been of immeasurable aid to great peoples in a day of transition. They have served magnificently their day and generation. Lands such as India and China are deeply in their debt, and much of Christian idealism has, through them, become incorporated into the standards of these and of other peoples. However, in the multitude of opportunities thus opened, any one of which could have absorbed all the time and all the funds available, the upbuilding of on-going Christian communities has become only one of several objectives.

However, we are now living in a day when such humanitarian tasks must more and more be performed, not by foreigners, but by those who are native born and reared. The rising tides of nationalism and of feeling against the white man's domination and the increasing possession of the techniques that have originated in the Occident make difficult the path of the stranger who leads in introducing new ways. If Christianity is to continue to be a source of beneficent enterprises, it must operate through Christian communities rooted in the soil. Yet in assisting these the foreigner can still be of service. The missionary is needed and greatly needed.

Another desirable change in missions is the flow of missionaries in more different directions. If the world-wide Christian fellowship is to become a growing reality, missionaries must go not only from the West to the East. They must also come from the East to the West, and they must be exchanged between various branches of the younger churches. Fortunately this has already begun. The great Japanese Christian, Kagawa, has gone on missions to the United States and Australia. T. Z. Koo is, fortunately, a name familiar to many in the United States. Not many years ago a "mission of help" came from the churches of India to the churches of Great Britain and Ireland to strengthen the latter by telling what the Christian experience has been meaning to the peoples of India. We have seen Negro Christians going from the United States to visit the Christians of India. For at least a generation to come the main flow of missionaries must be from the older and larger churches, which are mostly in the Occident, to the younger and smaller churches, which are generally in the non-Occidental world. The more, however, that missions flow in all directions between older and younger churches, between younger churches and younger churches, and between older churches and older churches, the more will all Christians be enriched and the more will the world-wide Christian fellowship become an actuality.

4. *The existing machinery for world-wide co-operation among Protestants must be strengthened and additional forms of co-operation must be encouraged.*

We have already seen how numerous are the agencies for this co-operation. It would be difficult to mention any one of these of any prominence that is not worthy of continued and vigorous life.

Particularly important because of its relations between the older and the younger churches is, as we have seen, the International Missionary Council and its affiliated regional councils. No other one set of agencies so provides a channel for that fellowship which is essential if the younger churches of the Protestant tradition are to come to that full stature which is essential to a fellowship that is world-wide. It is significant and highly encouraging that the enlarged meeting of the International Missionary Council planned for 1938 is to be held in India, an area wherein are some of the most important of the younger churches, that the emphasis of the meeting is to be on the Church, its life and message, and that fully half of the delegates are to be from the younger churches.

As we have repeatedly said, however, a world-wide Christian fellowship that is really inclusive is not to be obtained through any one organization. All bodies, old and new, which give promise of assisting toward that goal are to be encouraged.

5. *Collective approaches must be made by Christians toward the solution of some problems that cut across national lines.*

This will not be done by any one organization nor will all attempts be world-embracing. As samples of experiments that have already been made, one needs mention only the fact that in a number of ways Japanese and Chinese Christians have, through fellowship and action, been attempting to ease the chronic tension between their respective countries. So, too, the Agricultural Missions Foundation is endeavoring to mobilize the Christians of the world for the solution of some of the problems that make difficult the lives of those who till the soil, particularly in Asia and Africa.

Sometimes the efforts of Christians will call into existence bodies in which Christians and non-Christians co-operate toward a common end. For instance, the Institute of Pacific Relations was brought into being by Christians to aid in the amicable solution of international problems about the Pacific Basin. Naturally many Christians work through it. Naturally, too, many non-Christians who sympathize with its aims are also included.

6. *Ways must be devised to establish fellowship between members of the great historic divisions of the Christian movement—the Roman Catholic Church, the various Eastern churches, and the many Protestant bodies.*

Here organic union, as we have suggested, is out of the question. Even if it were desirable, which it probably is not, it is not feasible. Already, however, as we have seen, many friendly contacts exist on the basis of community of faith and of tasks that can be performed together. These can be multiplied. Here especially is a field for individual friendships. Wherever members of these communions are in geographic propinquity, those who see the opportunity can cultivate friendships with members of other branches of the faith—not with the purpose of changing the ecclesiastical allegiance of those friends, but with a desire to understand and to be understood, and to find, through fellowship, an enrichment of the Christian life of all. To some of us such friendships are among the most cherished of our memories. They have proved stimulating and enriching to a degree that we would not have thought possible. We have found, too, as we have attempted, somewhat timidly, to make such friendships that we have been met more than half way. Through them we have realized how much of real fellowship is possible through allegiance to a common Lord and how much communions other than our own have to contribute. Such friendships, multiplied, are of the essence of the world-wide Christian fellowship.

This group of suggestions may seem disappointing. They do not lead at once or even in one or two generations to the fully grown world-wide Christian fellowship that in our time is so desperately needed. Nor, even if it were realized, could one say "lo here, or lo there." It can never be identified with a visible structure.

Always, because of our nature, we are torn between two extremes. On the one hand is the desire to bring into actuality, in our own lifetime, the vision of the ages and to be impatient with delays. This is peculiarly the attitude of youth. In it is an element of selfishness and egotism—a desire to do what no one has yet achieved and a confidence that we are better than past generations and can succeed

where others have failed. In it, too, is much of fine un-
selfishness and of fresh, buoyant enthusiasm. On the other
hand is cynicism and despair—a realization of some of the
obstacles and a hopelessness of being able to overcome them.

To both extremes the Christian, if he but realizes it, has a
corrective at hand in his faith in God. The achievement of
the fellowship for which he longs rests, in the last analysis,
with God. God has given us enough of free will to enable
us to further—or to retard—the fulfilment of the dream, but
the dream, we believe, is first of all His and not ours, and
He has the ages through which to work. Because we believe
in Him we are saved from despair.

Moreover, in our own day we are seeing progress toward
that fellowship. Christians are now found in every land.
Organizational divisions have increased, but the longing for
an inclusive fellowship has grown. Means for making that
longing effective have multiplied. In spite of all the cleavages, we are approaching more closely to a true fellowship—
one which transcends organizations—than at any previous
time in Christian history. The world-wide Christian fellowship is not a mirage, ever vanishing as we think we are
approaching it, but a growing actuality. Ours is the high
privilege of contributing to its fuller realization.

A SELECTED BIBLIOGRAPHY

CONCRETE DESCRIPTIONS OF THE MISSIONARY ENTERPRISE

Axling, William. *Kagawa.* New York, Harper, 1932. $2.00.
A sympathetic biography and appraisal by an intimate friend.

Brockman, Fletcher S. *I Discover the Orient.* New York, Harper, 1935. $2.50.
An illuminating and intimate spiritual autobiography by a distinguished missionary to China, in his youth a leader in the Student Christian movement in the United States.

Fraser, Agnes R. *Donald Fraser of Livingstonia.* London, Hodder and Stoughton, 1934. $2.00.
An extraordinarily well written biography of one of the early leaders of the Student Christian Movement in Great Britain, later for many years a missionary in Africa.

Wilson, Jesse R., compiler and editor. *Men and Women of Far Horizons.* New York, Friendship Press, 1935. Cloth, $1.00; paper, $.60.
Made up of a number of vivid, first-hand concrete descriptions of current conditions, programs, and achievements of the missionary enterprise.

COMPREHENSIVE DESCRIPTIONS AND ANALYSES

The Christian Message for the World Today. New York, Round Table Press, 1934. $1.50.
By ten different authors.

Latourette, Kenneth Scott. *Missions Tomorrow.* New York, Harper, 1936. $2.00.
A comprehensive description of Christian missions of the past century and a quarter with a suggested program for the future.

Laymen's Foreign Missions Inquiry. Fact-Finders Reports. New York, Harper, 1933. 4 vols. $6.00.
Four volumes, dealing with India, Burma, China, Japan, home base, and missionary personnel. Detailed, objective studies by groups of technical observers.

Re-thinking Missions. New York, Harper, 1932. $2.00.
A much discussed volume, taking positive positions, written from the standpoint of liberal American Protestantism.

STATEMENTS OF THE REASONS FOR SUPPORTING CHRISTIAN MISSIONS

Paton, William. *A Faith for the World.* London, Edinburgh House Press, 1929. $.75.
By a secretary of the International Missionary Council, a former leader in the Student Christian Movement of Great Britain.

White, Hugh Vernon. *A Theology for Christian Missions.* Chicago, Willett, Clark, 1937. $2.50.

By a liberal Protestant evangelical, philosophically trained.

PERIODICALS

The International Review of Missions. 156 Fifth Avenue, New York City.

A quarterly. The most scholarly magazine dealing with missions.

World Christianity. A Digest. 140 South Dearborn St., Chicago.

A quarterly. Contains articles, book reviews, and digests of pertinent articles from several periodicals.